SPOTTER PUFF

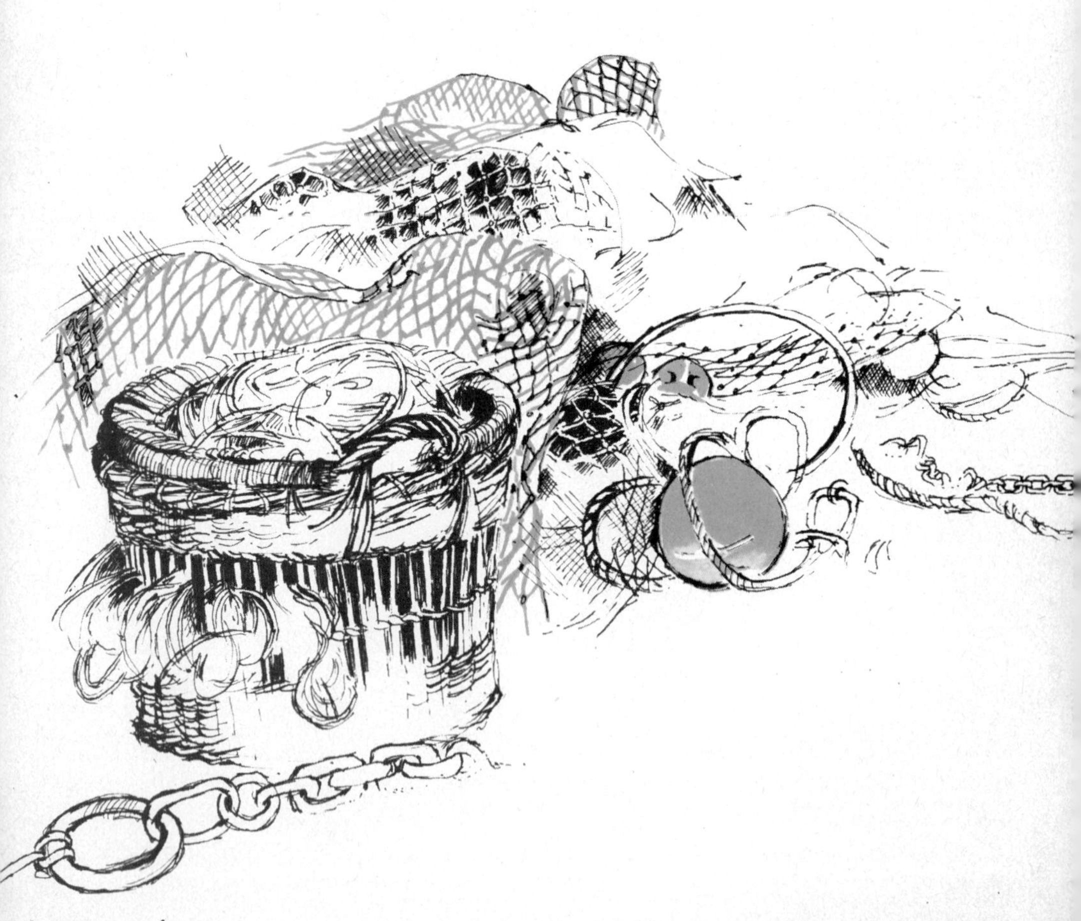

PUFFIN BOOKS

To my Father and Mother

In a wild place, within sound and smell of the sea, there was once a sandy hole. It sheltered beneath the grass on top of a tall cliff, while far below terrific waves burst against the rocks and flung spray up high into the air.

It looked like a rabbit hole, but a very different sort of family lived inside.

There was Puffred and his wife, Phoebe, and their son, Puff. Puff was rather small for his age but he was strong, and when he heard the waves dashing against the rocks he would feel excited and dream of dangerous fishing expeditions.

While Phoebe cleaned out their home, Puffred took Puff to another part of the cliff-top. Here there were many more holes and a great deal of activity. Older puffins greeted each other by bowing and rubbing bills and then they gathered together in a parliament. Spotter puffins had just come back from far out to sea.

'The best fish,' they announced, 'are in the North-west Sector.'

'Come,' said Puffred, and he took off into the breeze. Puff followed, and they flew out over the waves.

Suddenly Puffred swooped down and landed on the water with a splash. He dived and swam underneath using his wings and his paddles, and came up with a silver fish in his bill.

Puff copied his father. How he loved sea-diving. He was very proud of the fish he caught.

That night, as Puff lay inside the burrow, he thought about fishing and he longed for the morning. He wanted most of all to become a spotter puffin and bring back the important fishing news.

But while Puff lay curled up asleep the wind began to howl and whistle and moan. It gathered up great waves and flung them against the rocks until the whole cliff trembled.

At the height of the storm there was a terrible crash. The puffins woke up and peered out, frightened, into the darkness. They heard shouts and cries and bright lights flickered.

When dawn broke, an incredible sight met their eyes. Spotter puffins were sent out at once and the parliament anxiously awaited their return.

'There is a large black creature, larger than a whale,' they cried. 'He is crawling along beside the cliffs and stretching out to sea. But there are good fish further out.'

'Then that is where we must go,' said Puffred, taking off. Phoebe and Puff flew close behind him.

Puff wanted to see the black creature very much. There it was. It had more arms and legs than he could count and every time a wave rolled in the arms and legs swirled up and down.

'At least it hasn't got a mouth,' thought Puff, as he flew in to have a closer look. 'So it can't gobble me up.'

Puff flew much lower. The creature smelt very strange indeed. Suddenly he saw a large hole in the creature's middle. And through the hole Puff saw a fish.

Puff dived. But just as he did so the hole moved and Puff dived straight into the creature's back.

Poor Phoebe could not see her son anywhere. She hooted in alarm and circled above the monster. Then from below she heard a familiar squeak.

Thick black stuff held Puff fast. He tried hard to fly but he could not. Too frightened to land on the creature's back, Puffred and Phoebe swooped round calling encouragement. Puff lay very still with his bill in the air.

Puffred flew to fetch help while Phoebe stayed and watched miserably as her son was carried away. The big black creature held Puff fast and rode on the waves which rolled slowly towards the shore.

Puffred returned with some friends. But they just sat on a buoy and discussed the situation from a safe distance. Puffred and Phoebe bravely tried to scare the creature away but it would not let go of Puff.

Night fell, and to Phoebe the whole sea seemed full of the black creature and its unfamiliar smell. Puff floated off into the darkness.

He lay and watched the stars and tried to wiggle his paddles and move his wings. He struggled to preen his feathers but they tasted horrible. He felt hungry and he thought about all the fishes swimming far below him. He tried to look down but the black stuff smothered his face. That night was the blackest and longest that Puff had ever known.

By morning Puff found himself rolling over and over and then he felt hard sand beneath his back.

A little girl was walking along the beach looking for shells. Her father was a fisherman. When Puff saw her he was frightened and struggled to get back into the sea.

'Oh, you poor thing!' cried the little girl and she picked up Puff smearing black stuff all over herself.

Holding his wings carefully, she carried Puff back to the cottage where she lived.

'Look what I've found, Mother,' she said. 'A puffin's been caught in the oil.'

Puff was too tired to be frightened. But the little girl did not hurt him and neither did her mother. Puff watched all the black stuff disappear down a strange hole.

His wings felt better so he tried to flap them, and made rather a mess. Then he found that he could open his bill so he hooted a bit. He looked very shabby because the natural oil in his feathers had been washed away with the black stuff.

Then suddenly Puff began to feel terribly ill. He did not want any food. There was such a horrid smell and Puff wished that he could hear Phoebe calling. He closed his eyes.

The little girl wrapped him in a towel and sat with him by the fire. She stayed with him for hours and Puff hardly moved.

When it was time for her to go to bed, she put Puff in a basket and curled up by the fireside too.

Puff was so ill that he did not open his eyes until the little girl was having her breakfast next morning.

'Wherever am I?' he thought. Then he saw a fish hanging in the air. Puff opened his beak and the fish vanished, and then another, and another. Puff staggered to his feet.

'He'll get better now,' said a deep voice. Puff jumped. 'Oh, please don't be frightened,' said a smaller voice. Puff was not frightened of that voice.

During the following week. Puff learned many interesting things about the cottage and the three people who lived in it. As he grew stronger he hopped about the kitchen and he liked to play in the bath. He ate icy cold sprats and slept in a cardboard box.

Puffred and Phoebe came to visit him when when he was well enough to walk in the garden.

The little girl's father interested Puff most of all. He smelt deliciously of fish. Puff longed to go fishing, too, but the fisherman said, 'You've got to wait, little puffin, you've got to wait until your own oil comes back to your feathers. You're not water-tight and I'd never go to sea in a leaky boat myself.'

Puff hated waiting. He longed to fly and dive and swim in the sea. His paddles were really meant for swimming and they became sore with standing and walking. The little girl's mother gave Puff pills to make him feel stronger, but he was miserable away from the sea.

Then one day, after several months, when Puff had almost given up hope, the fisherman gave him a seaworthy test. And Puff floated!

Now at last Puff could go fishing again. He loved the old fishing boat which carried him out to sea. But what a complicated way to catch fish! Hours were spent just searching.

'What they need is a spotter puffin,' thought Puff.

So he kept a good look-out and when they were far out to sea he flew off.

He came back with a large fish in his bill. ‘That bird knows where to look,’ said the fisherman, and the next time Puff took off, the fishing boat followed him.

That night the fishing boat carried home a splendid catch.

So Puff stayed with the fisherman's family and became a very special spotter puffin. He would often visit Puffred and Phoebe to catch up on the news in the parliament. But never again did he dive when there was a large black creature about.